A.I.
ANCESTRAL INTELLIGENCE
Constellation Insights from Beyond

GARY STUART

ALSO BY GARY STUART

A.I.
ANCESTRAL INTELLIGENCE
Constellation Insights from Beyond

GARY STUART

ISBN: 9781090877260

DEDICATION

I want to dedicate this book to the greater "Consciousness of Totality" that connects us all.

All of my trusting and courageous clients that allowed me access to the entirety of their family lineage both living and dead. The honor was mine.

To all who attended my workshops who "donated their bodies to science" as client ancestor representatives. Their support and participation were invaluable. They expanded the healing awareness that taps into what's hidden (even from the working client), giving me the insights on a silver platter for all present.

My teachers Heinz Stark, Bert Hellinger, and many others. Their greatness inspired my desires and passion to learn from the best of the best.

My family of origin for teaching me the strength and tenacity I needed to survive them. The perfect training ground for what I needed to learn. I chose to excel in life with bravery and courage both taught to me in the deepest and wounding ways. There's HOPE!

My dearest Gary Corb, who spent his all too-short life supporting me and my dreams. I never thought this would be our fate and destiny as a couple. I know now more than ever, LOVE is ETERNAL.

I'm blessed beyond measure,
Namaste,
Gary Stuart

CONTENTS

FOREWORD

I was devastated and stunned that day. Even though I spoke to so many of my patients and counseled them on their grief from such a loss, I could not console myself. It was a beautiful Michigan day in July and I was enjoying it until I got a call from my sister and wife. "I think we lost him." was all I remembered. I was in shock and for a moment was paralyzed. My father, my hero, the man who taught me strength and courage, dedication and empathy was gone. Dr Uma Nandi lost his fight after a decades long struggle with complications from a devastating stroke. My world crumbled around me and for days I was in a daze, unable to withstand the pain. In honor of my beloved father, I shaved my head and spread his ashes in the running water, as so many Hindu sons had done for hundreds of years before me. My family was incredible...my rock in my time of sorrow.

I met Gary Stuart in Calgary, Canada earlier that year. Immediately, I loved his soul and understood how special he was. He introduced me to Ancestral Intelligence and I was part of an incredible constellation session led by Gary. He helped me understand how we really do stand on the shoulders of giants; in this case, the giants were our ancestors and their brilliance. When my father passed from my physical life, I called on Gary to help me in my quest for understanding my loss and for soul support. As always, Gary was incredible in his empathy, insight, warmth and kindness, for me and my family. He organized an event for me using ancestral intelligence through a constellation healing experience.

Through this constellation healing session, I was truly transformed to fully understand my loss, the death of my hero. Although I grieved, my insight and knowledge of the continuum of life was at a new level. Through ancestral intelligence, my family and I were able to take the grief of the loss and powerfully transform it into energy, empathy, and love.

Ancestral intelligence has been studied for centuries. Ancient civilizations have understood and revered this intelligence. Many of you have experienced it as the Chinese describe it, as chi, or the life force, present in all of us. In *Ancestral Intelligence*, Gary Stuart gives us the essence of what brings us together. He shows us that all life is consciousness and that this consciousness drives us all. Gary's journey into understanding this consciousness goes back two decades. Starting from his days as a stand-up comic, he has transformed his life and thousands of others with his teaching and wisdom.

He imparts this wisdom with love and respect, in a manner that is understandable and practical. In a world where many feel lost, without a true purpose or meaning, Gary's amazing work stands alone. Using his wit, humor, intelligence and empathy, he paves the way to achieve greatness despite losses. One thing is clear as Gary writes, "No matter how we currently express our choices or decisions in our lives, one thing is certain, we all share life and then die." Our choices can provide meaning for us and those who come after us; just as the choices of our ancestors provide meaning for us.

We face a crisis of loneliness in our technology savvy world. Although we can start our car with an app on our phone as we land on a plane, we can often struggle with our raison d'etre, our entire reason for existing. As a physician, a father, husband, son and brother, it tears my soul to hear of yet another suicide, another loss of life in this era where suicide occurs at an epidemic rate. I am shocked to hear of another death through opioid overdose, another beautiful soul lost so unnecessarily.

Ancestral Intelligence gives us a powerful glimpse of the entirety of life and consciousness. This wonderful work gives us tools to grapple with our own fears, our insecurities, and helps us utilize the wisdom of generations to discover our sweet souls. Never before have we needed these tools more than now, to discover ourselves through our ancestors and their wisdom and love.

I love this remarkable book and have great respect and admiration for its author Gary Stuart. In a planet longing for empathy, it stands alone in its quest to help us all discover our souls and our joy through the souls of our ancestors. Namaste!

Partha Nandi, MD FACP
CEO & Creator, The Dr Nandi Show, Emmy award winning television show
International Best-Selling Author
Ask Dr Nandi: 5 Steps to Becoming Your Own
#HealthHero for Longevity, Well-Being, and a Joyful Life
Detroit, Michigan 2019

PREFACE

Ancestral Intelligence is something we all share. No one would be alive to read this if it wasn't for our Ancestors. It's their skills and decisions that insured their survival and ours too. Each successive generation tends to judge their family of origin harshly. Many criticize that the forebears coulda, woulda, shoulda in a different way. Many often forget that all the choices they made had a positive impact. Their choices and fate allowed you to be born. This is how they shared the life you are now blessed with.

Life, in all its complexity supported them in achieving their greatness and longevity. History proves there is always an unseen emotional price. No matter how we currently express our choices or decisions in our lives, one thing is certain, we all share life and then die.

What makes Constellation messages and insights so great is the healing experience itself. Everyone has a second chance, we have a tool to re-experience or redo the past from an emotional and energetic point of view. What's even more ironic is that the dearly departed, or not so dearly departed, communicate intuitively and empathetically through the workshop attendees known as Representatives. These Reps objectively stand in for relatives living or dead. The working Constellation client then sees their subjective family system experience and its history more objectively. Chi (life force energy) can then move!

This book is a result of the thousands of Constellation insights and the deeper truths that I personally experienced. I've now facilitated over two decades of Constellation Healing Experiences for over 10,000 clients. It's a blessing from those deceased ancestors that helped birth this book. It's they who gifted me this deep, insightful wisdom experienced within the healing process known as Constellations. You could also say these insights and messages are part of an eternal feedback loop between Heaven and Earth plus the living and dead. Remember our physical DNA used to be theirs. Everyone has a direct connection to their Ancestors' time line whether they use it or not.

Think of your body as the physical hard drive connected to an ancestral cloud of limitless information. A universal/soul mind that's vaster than all the newly created A.I. that's in the world today, as we speak. Ancestral Intelligence contains all the information human history has ever experienced within our own family plus our entire species.

Today's Artificial Intelligence (A.I.) Revolution is brought to us by I.B.M. (Watson), Google, Amazon, Microsoft, and others. What all these technological giants don't seem to realize is that **life itself has its own algorithm**. It used to be called chi by the Chinese. Universal Life Force is older and wiser as it contains more wisdom than any computer-generated program could ever hope to artificially create. Maybe the whole Universe itself could be called a Cosmic Brain. We are all a part of it as each galaxy mirrors brain synapses that communicate both the seen and unseen simultaneously.

Ultimately, everything is consciousness. What I postulate is that consciousness has many messages plus incredible insights to share with the living and the world. All that is ever known or will be known already exists. It's our job to decipher the meaning and make it useful in our day-to-day experience. Information and instinct exist to be passed on to the next generation to ensure their survival. Ironically, you could say our species is a complete success even though it looks like a disaster in progress.

"Life doesn't care or look back it just moves forward."

Ancestral Intelligence is always forward moving. Fortunately, we get an opportunity to look back to learn and receive valuable information from everything that came before. Maybe the FUTURE reveals itself as you read this book. Once finished, it becomes your PAST yet hopefully it makes you wiser in the PRESENT.

A.I.
INSIGHTS

"We are
our ancestor's
dreams
come true."

"We cannot save
our ancestors
by suffering
in life."

"Suffering
in life
won't raise
the dead."

"Loyalty
to misery
is futile
&
unnecessary."

"Our ancestors
wanted
the same things
we want."

"Who else can master your universe but you?"

"The universe
is you,
as you are
the universe."

"There is no
good or bad,
just life lessons
to be learned."

"The attitude
of your
gratitude
equals true
empowerment."

"Adversity makes you stronger in order to face your future."

"The truth
never killed anyone
but lies
often do."

"Ultimately,
change
will do
you good."

"Your life
can change
in an
instant."

"Expanding consciousness beyond your beliefs creates growth."

"Conscious expansion
of limiting beliefs
creates brilliance."

"True healing
isn't just less suffering;
but having joy
and happiness
with ease."

"True healing
is more
than having
less suffering."

"Get back
to happy."

"You were more
than a pawn
in your parents'
chess game."

"Heaven
will always be there,
life will not.
Choose
accordingly."

"Respect & honor
are the most
important
keys to success."

"Loyalty & self-betrayal
to gain a mother's love
is dangerous
for the child."

"Finding harmony
with the past
is the quickest way
to future success."

"Honor life
and parents
for the biggest
rewards."

"Understand what
you know
&
know what
you understand."

"The greater the pain,
the deeper the love,
the stronger the bond."

"Life
is a
beautiful
nightmare."

"There's
no right,
no wrong,
just truth."

"Loving
imperfection
is
perfection."

"First comes thought,
then comes energy,
then comes matter."

"Life
has only
one goal,
move forward
at all cost."

"There is no death,
just a change of
dimension."

"If spirit moves you, move with spirit."

"What is hidden
wants to come
to light."

"The stronger
the charge,
the deeper
the bond."

"Life
is a gift,
use it wisely."

"There is
no past,
no present,
no future,
there's only now."

"Passionate hatred
is love
turned
inside out."

"There's no
destruction
only
transformation."

"Everything
is
consciousness."

"Life's lessons
are never
really lost,
only wisdom gained."

"Spirit unites,
religion
divides."

"Accept
the gift of life,
there is
no price to pay."

"Life will
test you
until you
trust it."

"Commit to inner peace first, then outer peace will follow."

"Death
is harder
on the living
than
on the departed."

"We all come from a long line of dead people."

"We dance from
spirit into life,
then from
death into spirit."

"Life is a temporary state, spirit is eternal."

"Death is forever,
life is now."

"Being alive
is the dream state,
wake up!"

"Life
is the opportunity
to activate your dreams
into reality."

"You survived
the nightmare,
now live
the dream."

"Once the past
is resolved,
the future
can be present."

"The universe
is all knowing
and all growing."

"To be born
is
to be lucky."

"The time
for a fresh start
is now."

"You deserve
a second chance,
and so does
everyone else.
Take it now!"

"Those dearest departed
are happiest when
we thrive on every level.
Then and only then
can they rest in peace."

"Unconditional love is
the most powerful
healing force
in existence."

"Acceptance
for what is,
allows memories
to recede
into the past."

"The road
to healing
is paved with
unconditional love."

"The paradox is,
the more we accept
we are helpless before
the forces of
life, sex, and death,
the more empowered
we become."

"Death
takes our choice away
and gives us
grief to fill the void."

"Death's secret weapon is the element of surprise."

"Death
is
rebirth
into
spirit."

"To know nothing,
is to
understand everything."

"There is no such thing
as negativity,
only a lack of
positive perception."

"Destruction
fuels
the wheel
of creation."

"Negative energy
is the catalyst
for positive change."

"Destructive forces
create
the equilibrium of life."

"Chaos is necessary
for the conditions
of change to emerge."

"Disintegration
needs chaos
to birth newness."

"Every
perpetrator
was a
victim first."

"Victims
are stronger,
perpetrators
are weaker."

"Suffering
is optional
and a choice."

"There is
no competition,
you've already won."

"Birth
initially feels
like death
to the fetus."

"Everyone
is powerless
to the
greater forces
of life and death."

"Life
is the teacher
and love
is the lesson."

"Life is a
dance between
giving & receiving."

"Life is like a snake
in green grass,
never looking back,
always moving
forward."

"God's mission
is to know herself
through her creation,
or to know himself
through his creation."

"The end
is the beginning
as the beginning
is the end."

"Life
is the most bloodthirsty,
amoral, ferocious force.
Everything is wired
to survive.
Life's only rule:
adapt or die."

"Truth
is a matter
of perception.
Lies
are a matter
of deception."

"The mind fails to comprehend, what the heart already knows."

"Once something
is whole,
it's no longer
a puzzle."

"Fear can
only thrive,
by the power
you give it."

"Feeling everything,
yet knowing nothing,
equals trust."

"Truth
is meaning
what you say
and saying
what you mean."

"The eternal spirit of change resides inside you."

"Your DNA
used to be your
ancestor's,
therefore
making you recycled."

"All the suffering
in the world
will not
return the dead
back to life."

"No one asked
for the life
they got."

"Codependency
replaces bonding
when real love
isn't present."

"Life
demands
resilience
&
tenacity."

"Death supports life,
as life supports death."

ABOUT
THE AUTHOR

Gary Stuart — Author, Founder, and Master Facilitator of the Constellation Healing Institute based in Rancho Mirage, California, continues to spread the healing messages and insights of Constellation Healing Experiences both home and abroad. His expertise includes speaking, consulting, and facilitating workshops.

His other Constellation books are available on Amazon; *Master YOUR Universe: How to Direct & Star in Your Own Life*, *Many Hearts, ONE SOUL*, and more.

He's the creator of Constellation Healing Oracle Cards available at **www.ConstellationHealingOracleCards.com**.

Gary is available for private readings, coaching, and Constellation Healing sessions in person at workshops or online. Book your appointment at **www.ConstellationHealingInstitute.com**.

You can catch Gary hosting *Conscious Connection with Gary Stuart* on Blog Talk Radio. He also appears on other progressive media outlets such as the popular *The Dr. Nandi Show* on ABC TV.

Made in the USA
San Bernardino, CA
15 August 2020